Here's all the great literature in this grade level of *Celebrate Reading!*

BOOK A

Once Upon a Hippo
Ways of Telling Stories

THREE UP A TREE

by James Marshall

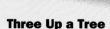

There's a Hole in the Bucket

pictures by Nadine Bernard Westcott

Hot Hippo
by Mwenye Hadithi
Illustrations by
Adrienne Kennaway
❋ KATE GREENAWAY
AUTHOR/ILLUSTRATOR MEDAL

Rosa and Blanca
retold by Joe Hayes
Illustrations by José Ortega

Featured Poets

Beatrice Schenk de Regniers
Ed Young

JIMMY LEE DID IT
BY PAT CUMMINGS

BOOK B

The Big Blank Piece of Paper

Artists at Work

Featured Poets

Dr. Seuss
Robert Louis Stevenson
Aileen Fisher
Tomie dePaola
Alonzo Lopez

BOOK C

You Be the Bread and I'll Be the Cheese

Showing How We Care

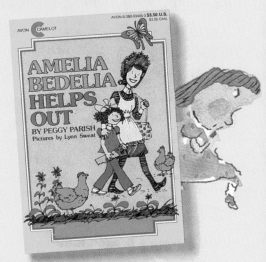
The Relatives Came
Story by CYNTHIA RYLANT   Illustrated by STEPHEN GAMMELL

Featured Poets

Mary Ann Hoberman
Charlotte Pomerantz

BOOK E

How to Talk to Bears

And Other Tips for Success

Under the Sunday Tree

Paintings by Mr. Amos Ferguson

...s by Eloise Greenfield

NESSA'S FISH

Oh No, It's Waylon's Birthday!

JAMES STEVENSON

BOOK F

Bathtub Voyages

Tales of Adventure

Featured Poets

John Ciardi
Sioux Indian Songs

Why Does Water Wiggle?
Learning About the World

Titles in This Set

Once Upon a Hippo
The Big Blank Piece of Paper
You Be the Bread and I'll Be the Cheese
Why Does Water Wiggle?
How to Talk to Bears
Bathtub Voyages

About the Cover Artist
Debbie Drechsler lives on a farm in California. She thinks
drawing is like making music. She likes to use colors the
same way an orchestra uses many different instruments to
make a song.

ISBN 0-673-80024-5

Copyright © 1993

Scott, Foresman and Company, Glenview, Illinois
All Rights Reserved.
Printed in the United States of America.

Acknowledgments appear on page 128.

5678910 VHJ 999897969594

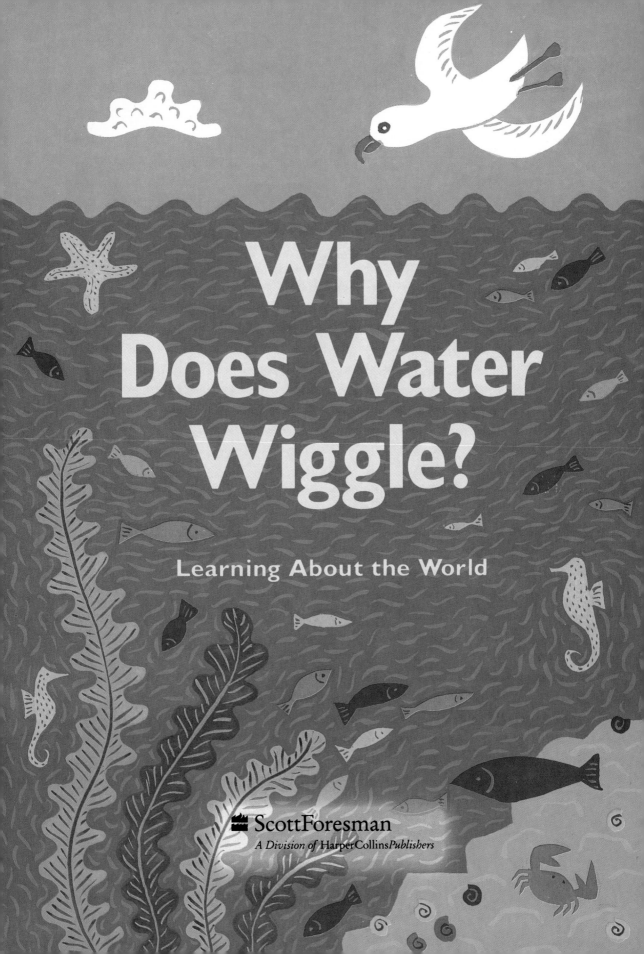

Why Does Water Wiggle?

Learning About the World

ScottForesman
A Division of HarperCollinsPublishers

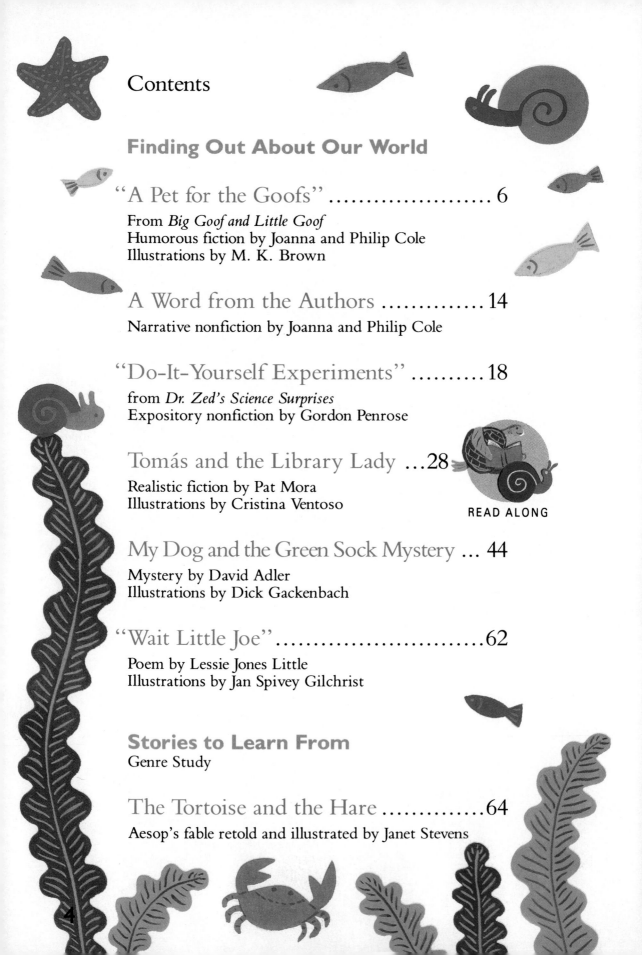

Contents

4

A PET FOR THE GOOFS

by Joanna and Philip Cole
illustrated by M. K. Brown

Big Goof and Little Goof lived together.
Sometimes they got everything all mixed up.
They were pretty goofy.

One day Big Goof and
Little Goof were working in
the yard when a turtle
walked by.

"Look at that cute little
animal!" said Little Goof.
"What is it?"

7

"I don't know," said Big Goof.

"We could keep it for a pet," said Little Goof.

"We never had a pet before," said Big Goof.
"We might do something wrong."

"We will read a book and learn how to take
care of it," said Little Goof.

8

The Goofs picked up the turtle and
walked to the library.

"Do you have a book on pets?"
Big Goof asked.

The librarian showed the Goofs a whole shelf
of books about pets. Big Goof picked one out.
It was called
OUR FRIEND THE DOG.

"*Dogs have four feet*," read Big Goof.

"One, two, three, four," counted Little Goof.
"Our pet has four feet. He is a dog!"

"*When a dog is happy, it wags its tail*,"
read Big Goof.

"Our dog has a tail, but he is not wagging it.
He must be sad," said Little Goof.

Big Goof read on, "*A dog needs a bone to chew and a collar to wear.*"

"No wonder our dog is sad," said Little Goof. "He doesn't have those things."

"Let's go get them right now," said Big Goof.

"Come on, Doggie," said Little Goof.

But the bone did not make Doggie wag his tail. Neither did the collar. The Goofs felt terrible.

Their pet was not happy. They walked around their yard wondering what to do.

When they passed the pond, Doggie jumped in and swam around. As he swam, his tail moved back and forth.

"Look at his tail!" cried Big Goof.

"He must be a water dog," said Little Goof. "He is happy when he is swimming."

Now when the weather is nice, the Goofs
take their dog for a swim in the pond.
When it is too cold or rainy to go out,
Doggie swims in the bathtub.

"We learned something, Little Goof,"
said Big Goof.

"Books don't tell you everything.
You have to find out some things
for yourself."

GOOFING AROUND: HOW WE INVENTED THE GOOFS

by Joanna and Philip Cole

Joanna Cole   Phil Cole

Hi! We are Joanna and Phil Cole. Together we wrote "A Pet for the Goofs."

We have a daughter named Rachel. Our family has six pets. We have a horse named Darwin, a dog named Muffy, and four guinea pigs— Isabel, Louise, Shirley, and Chuck. Can you guess which one is the boy guinea pig?

How can two people write a story together? After all, they cannot hold the same pencil. We wrote "A Pet for the Goofs" while we were driving in the car! Phil was behind the wheel. Joanna was next to him. She was the one holding the pencil. Rachel and Muffy were in the back seat.

15

Joanna said, "Let's think of a story about five goofy guys." Phil said, "Okay." Then we drove for a while and no one could think of anything. Then Phil said, "Five is too many. It should be two goofy guys." Joanna said, "How about Big Goof and Little Goof?"

"What will happen in the story?" asked Rachel. Muffy wanted to know too, but she can't talk.

"Maybe the Goofs should get a pet," said Joanna.

"Make it a turtle," said Rachel. Muffy wanted it to be a dog, but she can't talk.

Phil made up the first sentence: "One day Big Goof and Little Goof were working in the garden when a turtle walked by." Joanna wrote it down. Then Joanna thought of the next sentence, and so on.

In the end, we had a story about the Goofs and their pet turtle. Even though Muffy can't talk, we knew she wanted a dog in the story, so we put one in. Well, not really, but almost. If you've read the story, you know what we mean!

THINKING ABOUT IT

1. "What is that cute little animal?" Next time this happens, tell the Goofs how to find out.

2. Yes, a turtle is like a dog. How? No, a turtle is not like a dog. How? How would you explain this to the two Goofs?

3. The Goofs went to a museum. They saw a dinosaur. What do you think they said about it? Why?

More Goofy Tales

Are you interested in more "Goofy" adventures? You'll find them in *Big Goof and Little Goof!*

Do-It-Yourself Experiments

by Gordon Penrose

Body Tricks

**Surprise yourself with these body tricks.
Here's how:**

Hop Stopper

1 Bend over and grab your toes.

2 Keep your knees slightly bent.

3 Try to hop forward. Can you hop backward?

Balancing Act

1 Balance on one foot and count to ten.

2 Have a rest.

3 Balance on one foot again, this time with your eyes closed. What number can you count to before you fall over?

Quick! Which is bigger, your foot or your forearm?

Find out for sure by measuring your foot from heel to toe with a ruler or measuring tape. Then measure your arm from wrist to elbow. Were you right?

Fool your friends!

19

Fingerprints

True or false? All members of your family have the same fingerprints. Find the answer by collecting and comparing the fingerprints of your family and friends. Be sure to wash your hands before and after following these steps.

1 Lightly rub a thin coating of lipstick onto your fingertip.

2 Carefully place your smudged finger on a piece of clear Scotch tape.

3 Peel the tape off your finger and stick it onto a piece of clean paper.

Which fingerprint type is the most common?

Once you've collected prints of a number of people, compare them to each other and to these fingerprint types.

 **Arch**

 **Loop**

 **Whorl**

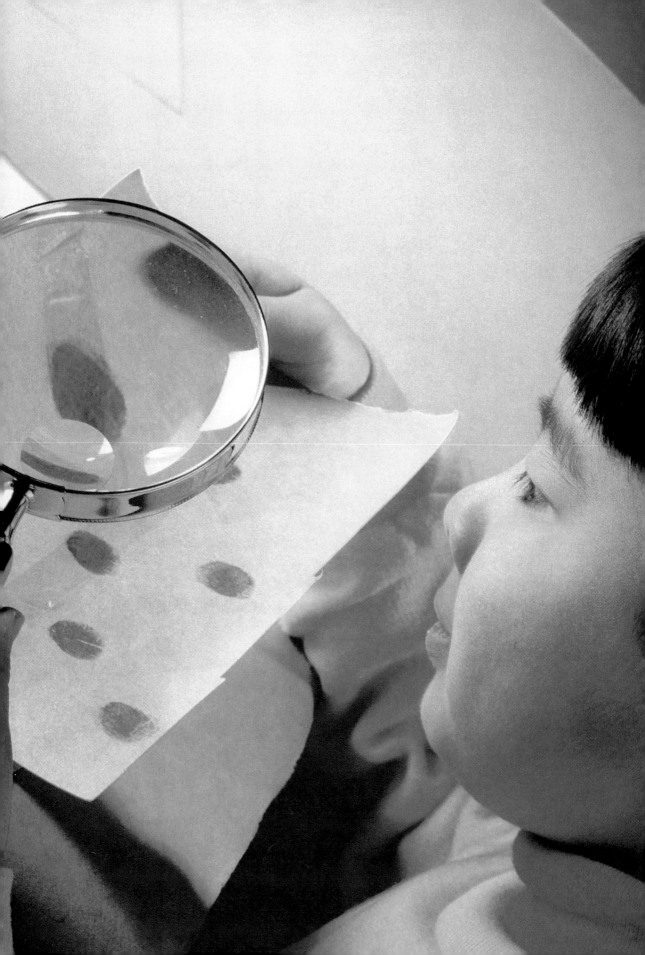

Lost and Found

Make a coin disappear right before your very eyes!

Here's how:

(1) Fill a glass with water.

(2) Put a coin in the palm of your hand.

(3) Place the glass on top of the coin and look down through it to see the coin.

(4) Now put your other hand on top of the glass and look for the coin through the side of the glass. Is it still there?

Try this pencil trick!

Put a pencil in a glass of water and look at it through the side of the glass. What happens to the pencil?

How did it break?

Elec-tricks

Your hair will stand on end when you try this trick! It works best on a dry day and with squeaky clean hair.

Here's how:

1 Rub a blown-up balloon back and forth on your hair.

2 Look into a mirror and slowly pull the balloon away from your head.

3 Watch your hair rise!

4 Now hold the balloon against a wall. When you let it go, does it stick to the wall?

Can a comb pick up paper? Yes! . . . if it's full of static electricity.

1 Run a plastic comb through your hair several times.

2 Hold the comb near small pieces of tissue paper or bits of paper towel.

3 Watch the paper jump!

You can make water wiggle without even touching it.

Turn on a cold water faucet and let the water flow in a slow, steady stream. Then run a plastic comb through your hair. Hold the comb beside the stream of water. What happens to the water when you move the comb back and forth?

Watch the water wiggle!

Thinking About It

1. Poof! It is important to follow instructions carefully when you do a science experiment. What other things do you do where it is important to follow instructions carefully?

2. Scientists must be careful when they do experiments and tell about them. How do Dr. Zed's experiments help you to be a good scientist?

3. Dr. Zed needs a helper! Think of another experiment that you could do. For example, how would you study toe prints? Explain why you'd like to do the experiment you plan.

Another Book of Science Experiments

Continue your scientific discoveries by trying the experiments in *Me and My Shadow* by Arthur Dorros.

Tomás and the Library Lady

by Pat Mora

illustrated by Cristina Ventoso

It was midnight. The light of the full moon followed the tired old truck. Tomás was tired too. Hot and tired. He missed his own bed in his own house in Texas.

Tomás was on his way to Iowa again with his family. His mother and father were farm workers. They picked fruit and vegetables for Texas farmers in the winter and for Iowa farmers in the summer. Year after year they bumped along in their rusty old truck.

"Mamá," whispered Tomás, "if I had a glass of cold water, I would drink it in large gulps. I would suck the ice. I would pour the last drops of water on my face."

Tomás was glad when the truck finally stopped. He helped his grandfather, Papá Grande, climb down. Tomás said, *"Buenas noches"*—"Good night"—to Papá, Mamá, Papá Grande, and to his little brother Henry. He curled up on the cot in the small house that his family shared with the other workers.

Early the next morning Mamá and Papá went out to pick corn in the green fields. All day they worked in the hot sun. Tomás and Henry carried water to them. Then the boys played with a ball Mamá had sewed from an old teddy bear.

When they got hot, they sat in the shade with Papá Grande. "Tell us the story about the man in the forest," said Tomás.

Tomás liked to listen to Papá Grande when he told stories in Spanish. Papá Grande was the best storyteller in the family.

"En un tiempo pasado," Papá Grande began. "Once upon a time . . . on a windy night a man was riding a horse through a forest. The wind was howling *whoooooooooo,* and the leaves were blowing, *whish, whish . . .*

"All of a sudden something grabbed the man. He couldn't move. He was too scared to look around. All night long he wanted to ride away. But he couldn't.

"How the wind howled, *whoooooooooo.* How the leaves blew. How his teeth chattered.

"Finally the sun came up. Slowly the man turned around. And who do you think was holding him?"

Tomás smiled and said, "A thorny tree."
Papá Grande laughed. "Tomás, you know all my stories," he said. "There are many more in the library. You are big enough to go by yourself. You can teach us new stories."

The next morning Tomás walked downtown. He looked at the big library. Its tall windows were like eyes glaring at him. Tomás walked around and around the big building. He saw children coming out carrying books. Slowly he started climbing up, up the steps. He counted them to himself in Spanish, *uno, dos, tres, cuatro.* . . . His mouth felt full of cotton.

Tomás stood in front of the library doors. He pressed his nose against the glass and peeked in. The library was huge!

A hand tapped his shoulder. Tomás jumped. A tall lady looked down at him. "It's a hot day," she said. "Come inside and have a drink of water. What's your name?" she asked.

"Tomás," he said.

"Come, Tomás," she said.

Inside it was cool. Tomás had never seen so many books. The lady watched him. "Come," she said, leading him to a drinking fountain. "First some water. Then I will bring books to this table for you. What would you like to read about?"

"Tigers. Dinosaurs," said Tomás.

Tomás drank the cold water. He looked at the tall ceiling. He looked at all the books around the room. He watched the lady take some books from the shelves and bring them to the table. "This chair is for you, Tomás," she said. Tomás sat down. Then very carefully he took a book from the pile and opened it.

Tomás saw dinosaurs bending their long necks to lap shiny water. He heard the cries of a wild snakebird. He felt the warm neck of the dinosaur as he held on tight for a ride. Tomás forgot about the library lady. He forgot about Iowa and Texas.

"Tomás, Tomás," said the library lady softly. Tomás looked around. The library was empty. The sun was setting.

The library lady looked at Tomás for a long time. She said, "Tomás, would you like to borrow two library books? I will check them out in my name."

Tomás walked out of the library carrying his books. He ran home, eager to show the new stories to his family.

Papá Grande looked at the library books. "Read to me," he said to Tomás. First Tomás showed him the pictures. He pointed to a tiger. "What a big tiger!" Tomás said first in English and then in Spanish, "*¡Qué tigre tan grande!*"

"Read to me in English," said Papá Grande. Tomás read about tiger eyes shining brightly in the jungle at night. He roared like a huge tiger. Papá, Mamá, and Henry laughed. They came and sat near him to hear his story.

Some days Tomás went with his parents to the dump. They looked for pieces of iron to sell in town. Henry looked for toys. Tomás looked for books. He would put the books in the sun to bake away the smell.

All summer, whenever he could, Tomás went to the library. The library lady would say, "First a drink of water and then some new books, Tomás."

On quiet days the library lady said, "Come to my desk and read to me, Tomás." Then she would say, "Please teach me some new words in Spanish."

Tomás would smile. He liked being the teacher. The library lady pointed to a book. "Book is *libro*," said Tomás. *"Libro,"* said the library lady.

"Pájaro," said Tomás, flapping his arms. The library lady laughed. "Bird," she said.

On days when the library was busy, Tomás read to himself. He'd look at the pictures for a long time. He smelled the smoke at an Indian camp. He rode a black horse across a hot, dusty desert. And in the evenings he would read the stories to Mamá, Papá, Papá Grande, and Henry.

One August afternoon Tomás brought Papá Grande to the library.

The library lady said, *"Buenas tardes, señor."* Tomás smiled. He had taught the library lady how to say "Good afternoon, sir" in Spanish. *"Buenas tardes, señora,"* Papá Grande replied.

Softly Tomás said, "I have a sad word to teach you today. The word is *adiós*. It means good-bye."

Tomás was going back to Texas. He would miss this quiet place, the cool water, the smooth, shiny books. He would miss the library lady.

"My mother sent this to thank you," said Tomás, handing her a small package. "It is *pan dulce*, sweet bread. My mother makes the best *pan dulce* in Texas."

The library lady said, "How nice. How very nice."

"Gracias, Tomás. Thank you." She gave Tomás a big hug.

That night, bumping along again in the tired old truck, Tomás held a shiny new book, a present from the library lady. Papá Grande smiled and said, "More stories for the new storyteller."

Tomás closed his eyes. He saw the dinosaurs drinking cool water long ago. He heard the cry of the wild snakebird. He felt the warm neck of the dinosaur as he held on tight for a bumpy ride.

Thinking About It

1. When Tomás reads books, he rides a black horse. He hears the cry of a snakebird. What happens to you when *you* read?

2. Back in Texas, Tomás gets books for his family. What books do you think he will get? Why will he choose them?

3. "You can teach us new stories." That's what Papá Grande tells Tomás. What new story would you like to teach to your family? Why?

Another Book About a Library Lady
In *Clara and the Bookwagon* by Nancy Smiler Levinson, Clara wants to learn to read more than anything. Will the bookwagon help her dream come true?

MY DOG and the GREEN SOCK MYSTERY

by David A. Adler
illustrated by Dick Gackenbach

My name is Jennie.

This is my dog.

My dog has white hair with black spots, a long tail and is really smart. She solves mysteries.

I couldn't think of a good name for my dog, so I just call her My Dog.

One afternoon I was outside playing with My Dog. I threw a ball across the yard. My Dog barked.

"Get it," I said. "Get the ball."

My Dog ran to the ball. But she ran past it. She ran out of my yard. When she didn't come back I went looking for her.

My Dog is smart but she gets lost a lot. I found My Dog running around my neighbor's house. She was looking for me.

I brought My Dog back to my yard. I was about to throw the ball again when I saw Andy.

"I need you to help me solve a mystery," Andy said. "Things have disappeared from my room. First it was my green sock. Then some baseball cards disappeared. And now my homework is gone."

My Dog barked. I knew what she wanted me to ask Andy. So I did.

"Where was your sock before it disappeared?" I asked.

"It was on my bed with all my other socks," Andy said. "I was just about to put them away."

My Dog barked again. She wanted to ask Andy where his baseball cards and homework were. But My Dog can't talk.

So I asked Andy, "Where were your baseball cards and homework?"

"My baseball cards were on my bed. My homework was on the floor on top of my book bag. I had just finished doing it. I went to the kitchen and had some milk and cookies. When I came back to my room the homework and baseball cards were gone. I need that homework," Andy said.

My Dog wagged her tail and barked.
I laughed. I knew what she wanted to say,
so I said it for her.

"My Dog has already solved your
mystery. Lots of kids are sloppy. Just clean
up your room and you'll find your things."

"Well, I'm not a sloppy kid," Andy
said. "My room doesn't need to be
cleaned up."

I looked at Andy. His shoelaces were
tied. His shirt and pants didn't have
wrinkles. He was right. He was not a
sloppy kid.

My Dog barked again. I told Andy, "My Dog says you must take us to your house. She will solve your mystery."

"Ha," Andy said. "Your dog doesn't solve mysteries. You do. Your dog is dumb."

"She is not," I told him.

"She's real dumb," Andy said. "I saw her chew a stick once. She thought it was a bone. And your dog is always getting lost."

I told Andy, "Just take us to your house. My Dog will prove she's smart. My Dog will solve your mystery."

As we walked, My Dog stopped at a trash can. The lid was off. My Dog put her head in and sniffed the trash.

I told Andy, "She's looking for clues."

"She's looking for a bone or a stick to eat," Andy said.

Before I walked into Andy's house, I wiped my feet. My Dog wiped her feet too, all four of them. As soon as we were inside, My Dog barked.

"Tell her to be quiet," Andy said. "My baby brother might be sleeping."

Andy's mother came out of the kitchen. A little boy was crawling behind her.

"You don't have to be quiet," Andy's mother said. "Billy isn't sleeping."

She went into the kitchen again. Billy followed her.

"Now come to my room," Andy said, "and I'll show you where I lost my green sock, my baseball cards and my homework."

Andy's room was really neat. On the shelves, little toy people, toy cars, and wooden blocks were standing in straight rows. I held onto My Dog. I didn't want her to mess up Andy's room.

"The homework was on the floor right on top of my book bag," Andy said. "And the sock and baseball cards were on my bed. I was just about to put them away."

There was nothing on Andy's floor, no papers, no pencils and no clothing. Andy really *is* neat.

I looked at his bed. It was covered with a blanket. My Dog barked. She wanted me to look under the blanket.

"I'm sorry," I told Andy as I pulled off the blanket, "but I have to do this."

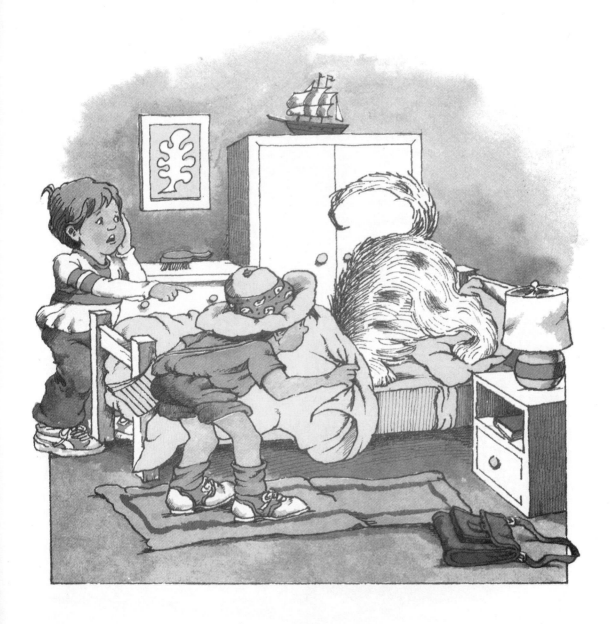

Under the blanket was a sheet. I pulled off the sheet and found another sheet. I pulled that one off too. But I didn't find the green sock, the baseball cards or the missing homework.

"Look what you did to my bed," Andy said. He began to put the sheets back on the bed.

Billy crawled into Andy's room. He was holding a piece of bread. My Dog barked.

"Keep that dog away from my brother," Andy said as he picked up Billy.

My Dog barked again. She pulled
away from me and jumped at the bread.
My Dog knocked over the desk chair.
The toy people, cars and blocks fell off
the shelves.

"Look what your dog did," Andy said.
He put Billy down. Then Andy began to
pick up the toys.

Billy crawled out of the room. I
grabbed My Dog's collar before she could
chase after Billy.

My Dog pulled me out into the hall.
Billy was there. We followed him to a
room with a crib and lots of baby toys.

"This must be Billy's room," I told
My Dog.

Billy crawled to his crib. He put the bread under the crib. Then he crawled to his toys and began to play with them.

My Dog pulled away from me. She put her head under Billy's crib and pulled out the bread. My Dog ate the bread. Then she put her head under the crib and pulled out another piece of bread and a green sock.

I looked under Billy's crib. I found a slipper, a torn book, a mitten and a spoon. I also found baseball cards and Andy's homework.

"Hey Andy!" I called. "My Dog has done it again. My Dog has solved your mystery."

When Andy came into Billy's room, I showed him Billy's hiding place and all the things he had there. And then I said, "My Dog isn't dumb. My Dog has solved your mystery."

Andy picked up his sock, his baseball cards and his homework. Then he looked at My Dog. She was still eating the bread.

Andy said, "Maybe your dog is smart. Or maybe your dog is dumb and just likes to eat bread."

When we left Andy's house, My Dog ran ahead. When I got home My Dog wasn't there, so I went looking for My Dog. She was lost again.

THINKING ABOUT IT

1. Do things ever disappear around your house? How do you solve mysteries without My Dog?

2. Andy isn't sure if My Dog is smart, or if she is dumb and just likes bread. What do *you* think? Why?

3. Jennie and Andy's neighborhood is having a picnic. How do you think My Dog will behave at the picnic? Why?

Another Book About My Dog

Jennie and My Dog try to find a missing bicycle in *My Dog and the Birthday Mystery* by David A. Adler.

Wait Little Joe

by Lessie Jones Little

"That ditch is too wide," I told Little Joe.
"Thomas is ten, you're only four, you know."

"I can jump that ditch," said Little Joe,
So he pitched himself as far as he could go,
But he missed the mark and landed in the middle!
And he knew at once that he was too little.

Bill fished him out and made him promise
That he wouldn't jump again
    till he was big as Thomas.

The Tortoise
and the Hare

An Aesop Fable
retold and illustrated by
Janet Stevens

Once upon a time, there was a tortoise and a hare.

Tortoise was friendly and quiet. He did everything slowly. Hare was flashy and rude. He did everything quickly.

Hare liked to tease Tortoise about being so slow.

When Tortoise ate breakfast, Hare said, "By the time you finish your last bite, it will be dinnertime."

When Tortoise worked in his garden, Hare said, "By the time you pick those spring flowers, it will be winter."

One afternoon, Hare followed Tortoise to
the store. Hare teased him on the way. "By the time
you get there, the store will be closed," he said.
"You're so slow, I could beat you at a race, hopping
backwards on one paw."

"But I could never beat you, Hare," said
Tortoise.

"Yes, you could," said Tortoise's friends. "All
you need is a little help."

"Then you *will* race me, Tortoise?" asked Hare.

Tortoise pulled his head into his shell.

"I don't want to," he said.

"You've got to," said his friends. "You've put up with that nasty hare long enough. We think you can win."

Tortoise didn't want to disappoint his friends, so he finally agreed to race against Hare.

Tortoise only had two-and-a-half weeks to get in shape before the big race. Rooster helped him out at the gym. Raccoon cooked him healthy meals.

Frog went jogging with him every morning.
By the day of the race, Tortoise was ready.

Animals from all over the county came to watch the tortoise and the hare.

Rooster read aloud the rules and described the course.

"Attention, everyone. The race will begin when I sound this gong. The six-mile course is marked by red flags. The first one to reach the finish line wins. Runners, take your mark, get set, GO!!" Raccoon sounded the gong.

Hare bolted out of sight before Tortoise had taken his first step. The crowd roared and cheered as Tortoise inched forward.

Hare was so far ahead that he decided to stop at Bear's house for something cool to drink.

Hare rested and sipped lemonade. Bear noticed something moving outside the window. "Hare, there goes Tortoise."

"What?" yelled Hare, running out the door.

Hare passed Tortoise for the second time. Then he decided to stop at Mouse's house for a snack.

As Hare munched on crackers and cheese, Mouse yelled, "Is that Tortoise I see out the window?"

"I'm not worried about that slowpoke," said Hare. "I've passed him twice already." Then he finished his snack and hopped out the door.

Hare passed Tortoise for a third time. Now, he was far ahead. He saw a pond and decided to stop and rest. The snacks had made him sleepy.

Hare was so sure that he would win, he took a nap in the soft grass. As he closed his eyes, he dreamed of victory.

Suddenly, Hare woke up because the crowd
was cheering.

"Yay, Tortoise," the crowd roared.

Tortoise was two steps away from the finish line.

"Slow down, you bowlegged reptile," screamed
Hare as he tried to catch up.

But it was too late. Tortoise crossed the line just before the tornado of dust and fur that was Hare flew by. Tortoise had won the race. Hare couldn't believe it. That measly shell on legs had beaten him.

TORTOISE

Tortoise smiled as his friends carried him on
their shoulders. He had learned an important lesson:

HARD WORK AND PERSEVERANCE BRING REWARD.

With Wrinkles and All

by Janet Stevens

Janet Stevens

When I was a child, I loved fables. My mom used to read fables like *The Tortoise and the Hare* to me. They had very few pictures. As she read to me, I remember painting pictures of the stories in my head.

Today, I draw pictures for stories that other people have written. Sometimes I illustrate the very old stories that I enjoyed as a little girl. I love to draw the animals in the stories, especially the ones with wrinkles. My favorite animal to draw is a rhinoceros, because it has *lots* of wrinkles. I also like to draw walruses and turtles. You probably know why! Rabbits are my favorite "non-wrinkly" animal to draw.

The race in *The Tortoise and the Hare* first attracted me to the story. When I thought of illustrating this fable as a book, it seemed to me that everyone was jogging. I even started jogging!

"What a perfect story," I thought. My Tortoise could practice like I do! He would be like me, not too fast but willing to put in some hard work. My Tortoise would lift weights, eat healthful food, and practice running.

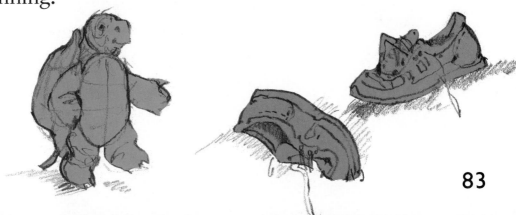

I really liked drawing that wrinkly Tortoise. His expressions were fun to draw on his wrinkle-filled face. For Hare, I thought of the scraggly jackrabbits on my grandfather's Texas ranch. They always seemed so sassy, sure of themselves, and ready to race at the drop of a hat.

I used many things around my house in this story. The Tortoise is wearing my daughter's bunny slippers. Hare is wearing my husband's pink tie! Of course Tortoise wears *my* running shoes, and Hare has on *my* running shorts.

I tested out *The Tortoise and the Hare* on my children. They liked the action in my drawings and were happy to see their own things in the book. It is always important to my daughter that I draw what the words say. My son likes to laugh and to see scary things in my books.

I love turning tales like *The Tortoise and the Hare* into books for children today. When I was a child, the animals in fables made me smile and taught me important lessons at the same time. Now I'm happy when one of *you* reads the story, giggles, and perhaps learns what our friend Tortoise has learned.

Thinking About It

1. Tortoise wins! But Tortoise didn't think he could beat Hare in the race. What have you done that you didn't think you could do? Explain.

2. Hare was fast, but he lost the race to Tortoise. What advice would a coach give Hare about his next race? Why?

3. Poor Hare went back to Mouse's house for dinner. What did he tell her about his *next* race? Why do you think so?

Another Book by Janet Stevens

What's better: city life or country life? Find out in *The Town Mouse and The Country Mouse.*

The Monkey and The Pea

retold by Nancy Ross Ryan
illustrated by Krystyna Stasiak

Long ago in India, a greedy little monkey lived in a tree in the king's park. If the monkey had one banana, he popped the whole thing into his mouth. If he had two bananas, he gobbled one first, then the other, as fast as he could. And if he had three bananas, he stuffed one in his mouth and held onto the others, one in each hand. The more food there was, the faster he ate.

One day the king was walking in the park with his son, the prince. They stopped by the stable to feed the royal horses. The prince had some fresh green peas for the horses as a special treat.

From his tree the little monkey saw the peas. He jumped down and grabbed a handful of peas. Then he climbed back up to the top and sat on a branch to eat them. When he opened his hand to eat, one pea, just one pea, fell from his hand down to the ground.

Oh! How upset the monkey was. He jumped up and down in the tree. He yelled and he cried. He squeaked and he shrieked. He howled, he yowled, and he bawled.

He ran back down the tree to find the lost pea. In his hurry, he dropped the other peas from his hand. They fell to the ground and rolled away.

The little monkey looked to the left. He looked to the right. He looked in the grass. He looked in the bushes. He looked high and low.

But he could not find the lost pea. He could not find any of the other peas either. He had lost them, one and all.

By now the horses had eaten all their peas. Not one pea was left.

The prince laughed at the little monkey. But the king said:

Let that greedy monkey be
A lesson, son, for you and me:
He lost a handful needlessly
By chasing after one small pea.

The Big Fish Who Wasn't So Big

retold by Julius Lester
illustrated by Karen Barbour

Once there was a pond next to a river. In the pond lived many small fish. They were not very happy, however, because a BIG fish also lived in the pond.

The BIG fish was not bad. It simply thought it was better and more important because it was BIGGER. When small fish swam too close, it announced, "Stop making those tiny waves. I can't sleep. A BIG fish like me needs more sleep than you little puny fish."

One day a small fish grew tired of hearing how unimportant it was. "Why don't you go swim with all the other BIG fish in the river?" it suggested. "You will be among fish as important as you are."

That was the best idea the BIG fish had ever heard.

Soon the rains of spring began. The river flowed over its banks and into the pond. It was easy for the BIG fish to swim into the river.

At once, the BIG fish noticed something. Everything was BIGGER than it was.

The rocks on the floor of the river were

ENORMOUS.

The water in the river flowed swiftly and with much strength. And the other fish? They were

HUGE,   HUGER,

and HUGEST!

Something bit its tail. The BIG fish turned to see the ugly face of a HUGE tiger fish, its mouth open, ready to eat the BIG fish with one gulp!

93

The BIG fish swam quickly behind a large rock and hid. It didn't feel BIG now. It felt small and very afraid. All it wanted was to swim back to the pond where it was quiet and peaceful. And that's what it did.

After that day, the big fish played with the little fish and took them for rides on its back.

No matter how big we are, we need to learn how to live with everyone.

Thinking About It

1. BIG Fish thought BIGGER was better. When would you agree with him? When do you think smaller is better? Why?

2. Are you a fable fan? How are the three fables you read alike? How are they different?

3. Greedy monkey is coming to dinner at your house! What advice will you give him about table manners? Why?

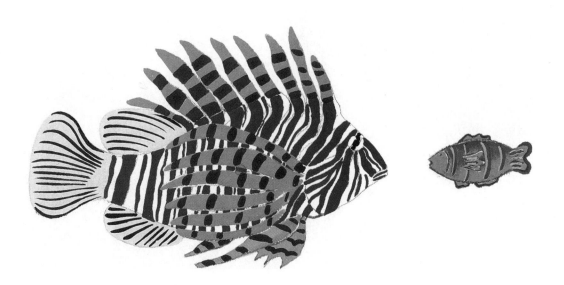

Animal Babies

by Jane Burton

Animals know some things by instinct. That is, they are born knowing certain things. A baby chick is born hungry, and it already knows to peck at any small, hard, shiny object. It knows *how* to eat, but not *what* to eat. Soon it learns to peck at seeds instead of another chick's beak!

A baby horse—called a foal—gets all the food it needs from its mother. The foal has plenty of time between meals for exploring. It looks and listens, smells and touches, learning all the time. The foal tastes everything—grass and earth and the bark of a tree—learning what things to eat and what *not* to eat.

When puppies are not eating or sleeping, they are usually romping. It looks as if they are just having fun, but they are also learning all kinds of important things through play.

Puppies chew to help their teeth and jaws grow strong. When one pup has a stick, the others all want the same one. Friendly squabbles help them learn about each other—who is bossy, who is gentle—and how to get along together when they are grown up.

It never takes long for some wild animals to discover new places where they can find food. A brown bear will eat all kinds of things in the wild, such as berries and shoots, salmon and birds' eggs. But bears also learn to like the sandwiches, potato chips, and hamburgers that people leave for them at picnic sites.

Dolphins eat only fish. They are very intelligent and quickly learn to perform clever tricks, such as leaping through hoops and playing basketball. They have learned that after each trick there will be a fishy reward!

Thinking About It

1. Amazing! What did you learn about animals that you didn't know before?

2. What things do baby animals and baby people both have to learn? How do they learn them?

3. What baby animal would you like to study? The koala? The chimpanzee? What would you like to learn about this baby animal?

Another Book About Animals

Ducklings, by Kate Petty, tells how ducklings learn to swim, gather food, and even "talk" to each other.

Robin spied a chubby worm
and thought he'd have a snack,
but when he tried to tug that worm,
it rudely tugged him back.

The worm was strong and sturdy,
and it pulled him off his feet,
so Robin thought he'd better find
a smaller worm to eat.

by Jack Prelutsky
illustrated by Garth Williams

Buffy's Orange Leash

by Stephen Golder and Lise Memling
illustrated by Michele Warner

Buffy is a furry white dog who lives with the Johnson family.

Buffy lives with Mr. Johnson, Mrs. Johnson, and little Billy Johnson. The Johnsons are not ordinary people. Can you guess what makes the Johnson family a little bit different?

Mr. and Mrs. Johnson can't hear—they are deaf. They can't hear any sounds. They can't hear the telephone or the doorbell ringing, the kettle whistling, or Billy crying.

The Johnsons are not able to hear, but they certainly can talk. They use their hands to talk in sign language.

Buffy is not an ordinary dog. He is a Hearing Dog. He uses his ears to help Mr. and Mrs. Johnson hear important sounds in their home.

Buffy also understands five signs that the Johnsons use when they talk to him.

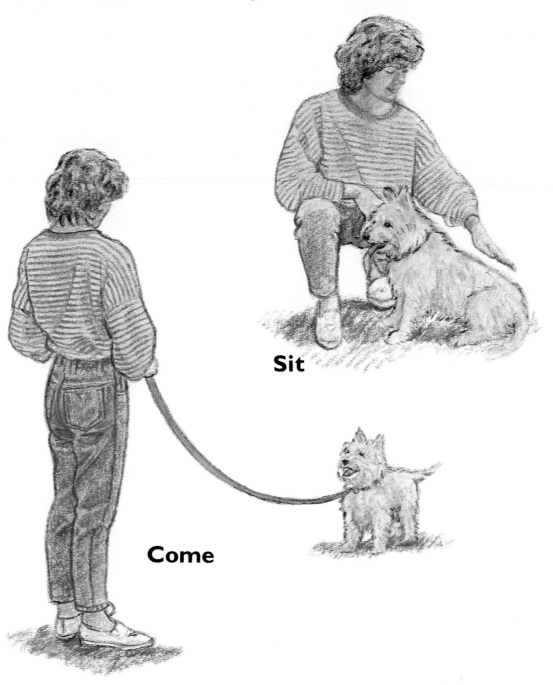

Sit

Come

Heel

Stay

Down

When Buffy was young, he lived in a kennel. One day, two people from the Red Acre Farm Hearing Dog Center visited the kennel. They looked at many different dogs. They chose Buffy to be a Hearing Dog. Why did they choose him? Buffy was friendly.

Buffy was smart. And Buffy liked to listen. He was more interested in listening than in looking or sniffing.

The Hearing Dog trainers took Buffy from the kennel. They brought him to Red Acre Farm Hearing Dog Center. Red Acre Farm is a school that teaches dogs to help deaf people.

The trainers taught Buffy how to listen for certain sounds, like the doorbell and the telephone.

When Buffy finished school, his trainers gave him an orange leash and collar. All Hearing Dogs from Red Acre Farm wear an orange leash and collar.

The trainers also gave Mr. and Mrs. Johnson a card with Buffy's picture on it. This card tells everyone that Buffy is a Hearing Dog.

At school Buffy learned many ways to help the Johnsons. When the telephone rings, Buffy runs over and touches the Johnsons and leads them to their telephone.

The Johnsons have a special telephone because they can't hear people talking. Their telephone looks like a typewriter. It is called a TDD. The TDD lets the Johnsons type their conversations over the telephone.

Buffy listens for many sounds. When he hears someone ring the doorbell or knock on the door, he touches the Johnsons and leads them to the door.

Buffy learned to wake up Mr. and Mrs. Johnson. When the alarm clock goes off in the morning, Buffy jumps up on the bed.

Buffy nudges the Johnsons until they wake up. Then they get up and give Billy his breakfast and get ready for work.

Buffy does other jobs, too. One of Buffy's other jobs is to listen for Billy.

When Billy cries or makes noise, Buffy runs over to Mr. or Mrs. Johnson. He leads one of them over to Billy.

Buffy's most important job is to warn the Johnsons when the smoke detector goes off. The Johnsons can't hear it, so they need Buffy to tell them when it beeps.

Buffy runs over and touches the Johnsons and then quickly drops to the floor when he hears the beep. That is how he tells them there is a fire.

The Johnsons love Buffy and pet him all the time, especially right after he helps them. When they pet Buffy, it helps him to remember his hearing jobs. Buffy is an important member of the Johnson family.

Buffy can go wherever the Johnsons go. He wears his bright orange leash and collar. The special leash and collar tell people that he is a Hearing Dog that helps deaf people.

Now you know what a Hearing Dog is. One day you may see Buffy or another Hearing Dog helping a deaf person. Then, you can tell your friends all about Buffy's orange leash.

Pulling It All Together

1. If you couldn't hear, how could Buffy help you? What new things would you want Buffy to learn to do?

2. Your teacher has asked you to do a report on your favorite animal. Which character or author from this book would you ask for help? Why?

3. A spaceship has landed! What would each of these characters do to learn about it—the Goofs, Tomás, and Jennie and My Dog? Why?

Books to Enjoy

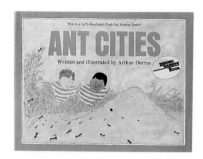

Ant Cities

Written and illustrated by
Arthur Dorros

Did you know ants build "cities"?
This book gives you directions on
how you can watch ants at work.

Greg's Microscope

by Millicent E. Selsam
Illustrations by Arnold Lobel

When Greg gets a new microscope,
nothing in his home looks the same.

An Octopus Is Amazing

by Patricia Lauber

Did you know that an octopus can
change colors? This eight-legged,
playful sea creature does other
amazing things too.

Once In A Wood:
Ten Tales from Aesop
Retold and illustrated by Eve Rice

Some lessons are learned the hard
way in "The Fox and the Goat,"
"The Fox and the Crow," and eight
other famous fables by Aesop.

My Dog and the Key Mystery
by David A. Adler

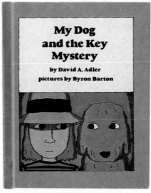

When Susan loses her key, Jennie
and My Dog have another mystery
to solve.

Something Queer at the
Lemonade Stand
by Elizabeth Levy
Illustrations by Mordicai Gerstein

Someone is trying to ruin Jill and
Gwen's lemonade business.
Who would do this? And why?

Literary Terms

Characters

Characters are the people or animals in the story. Sometimes we learn about a character through what other characters say. What did you learn about My Dog in *My Dog and the Green Sock Mystery?*

Fable

A **fable** is a short story that teaches a lesson. The characters are often animals. *The Monkey and the Pea* is a fable.

Moral

The lesson that is taught in a fable is the **moral.** The moral usually tells us how to be a better person.

No matter how big we are, we have to learn how to live with everyone.

Mystery

A **mystery** is a story about strange, unexplained events. The characters try to solve the mystery by finding clues. Jenny looks for clues to solve the mystery in *My Dog and the Green Sock Mystery.*

Nonfiction

Nonfiction is a kind of writing that tells about real people or things. *Buffy's Orange Leash* tells facts about Hearing Dogs.

Plot

The **plot** is what happens in a story. In a mystery, each event in the plot helps you to solve the mystery and figure out how the story will end.

Glossary

Words from your stories

collar

enormous

bor•row to get something from a person just for a while: *He borrowed my book and promised to give it back.* **borrowed, borrowing.**

col•lar a band that is put around the neck of a dog or other pet. *My dog's collar has her name on it.* **collars.**

com•pare to tell how people or things are alike and how they are different: *The boys compared their lunches.* **compared, comparing.**

dis•ap•pear to go out of sight: *The birds disappeared in the clouds.* **disappeared, disappearing.**

dis•cov•er to find out; see or learn of for the first time: *He discovered tiny insects living under the stone.* **discovered, discovering.**

e•nor•mous very, very large: *We saw an enormous hippo at the zoo.*

ex•plore   to go over a place carefully; examine: *The children explored the new playground.* **explored, exploring.**

fau•cet   something for turning on or off a flow of water from a pipe: *Is this faucet for cold or hot water?* **faucets.**

faucet

fin•ger•print   a mark made by the tip of a finger: *Whose fingerprints are on the mirror?* **fingerprints.**

flash•y   bright; likely to attract attention: *His coat was too flashy.* **flashier, flashiest.**

fore•arm   the part of the arm between the elbow and the wrist: *Celie got sunburned on her forearms.* **forearms.**

gob•ble   to eat fast and noisily: *The hungry dog gobbled his dinner.* **gobbled, gobbling.**

fingerprint

goof•y   silly; foolish: *When Stan puts his shoes on his hands, he is acting goofy.* **goofier, goofiest.**

greed•y   wanting more than your share: *Help yourself to candy, but don't be greedy.* **greedier, greediest.**

huge   very large in size or amount: *An elephant is a huge animal.* **huger, hugest.**

123

im·por·tant   having great meaning or value. *It is important that you learn to read.*

in·stinct   a way of acting that someone is born with: *Baby ducks are born with the instinct to follow their mother.* **instincts.**

in·tel·li·gent   able to learn; quick at learning: *Humans and other animals are intelligent creatures.*

li·brar·i·an   a person who directs or helps to manage a library: *We asked the librarian for a book on stars.* **librarians.**

meas·ur·ing tape   a long strip of cloth or metal, marked in feet or meters, used for measuring: *Use the measuring tape to see how big your bedroom is.* **measuring tapes.**

measuring tape

need·less·ly   without being necessary; in a wasted manner: *He risked his hurt leg needlessly in the race.*

ob·ject   anything solid that you can see or touch. *The objects on my desk are a pen and a book.* **objects.**

objects

or•di•nar•y usual or regular: *My ordinary lunch time is noon.*

peace•ful quiet; calm; full of peace: *The night was peaceful after the noisy storm.*

per•form to act, sing, play, or do tricks in public: *Clowns performed in the circus.* **performed, performing.**

perform

per•se•ver•ance sticking to a task or a goal; never giving up: *Her perseverance helped her learn to swim.*

pu•ny weak; small: *The puppy was so puny I could hold it in my hand.* **punier, puniest.**

re•ward something you get in return for something you have done: *A trip to the space show was our reward for raking all the leaves.* **rewards.**

romp to play in a rough, tumbling way: *The children were romping on the lawn.* **romped, romping.**

rude with bad manners; not polite: *My brother was rude and didn't say hello to my best friend.* **ruder, rudest.**

romp

125

sign language

sloppy

sign lan•guage   a way of talking that uses motions of the hands: *The students at the school for the deaf were talking in sign language.*

slop•py   not neat; untidy: *Van liked to dress in sloppy clothes when he cleaned the garage.* **sloppier, sloppiest.**

slow•poke   a very slow person or creature: *My brother is a slowpoke who is always late.* **slowpokes.**

smoke de•tec•tor   something that sounds an alarm when it senses smoke or fire: *Smoke detectors are used in homes and businesses to warn of fire.* **smoke detectors.**

smudge   to mark with dirt or ink; smear: *My gloves were smudged after I worked in the garden.* **smudged, smudging.**

solve   to find the answer to something: *The detective solved the mystery by using several good clues.* **solved, solving.**

squab•ble   a noisy fight: *We squabbled over which movie to see.* **squabbled, squabbling.**

stat•ic e•lec•tric•i•ty   a form of energy that builds up on objects which rub against each other: *Susan's hair crackled with static electricity when she brushed it.*

ter·ri·ble causing great fear; awful: *The terrible storm destroyed many homes.*

thorn·y when a plant or tree is filled with sharp points: *I caught my shirt on a thorny bush.* **thornier, thorniest.**

train·er a person who trains people or animals: *Melissa has a trainer to help her prepare for long races.* **trainers.**

thorny

un·im·por·tant not important: *My sister thinks my ideas are unimportant.* See **important.**

up·set very unhappy; greatly disturbed: *She was upset when her dog ran away.*

vic·tor·y the winning of a game or other contest: *Our team had another victory last night.* **victories.**

won·der a strange and surprising thing or event: *It's a wonder that you found us in this big crowd.* **wonders.**

wrin·kle a fold on the surface of something that is usually flat: *She used the iron to press out the wrinkles in her dress.* **wrinkles, wrinkled.**

wrinkle

Acknowledgments

Text

Page 6: "A Pet for the Goofs" from *Big Goof and Little Goof* by Joanna and Philip Cole. Illustrated by M. K. Brown. Text copyright © 1989 by Joanna and Philip Cole. Illustrations copyright © 1989 by M. K. Brown. Reprinted by permission of Scholastic Inc.

Page 14: "Goofing Around: How We Invented the Goofs," by Joanna and Philip Cole. Copyright © by Joanna and Philip Cole, 1991. Illustrations from *Big Goof and Little Goof* by Joanna and Philip Cole, illustrated by M. K. Brown. Illustrations copyright © 1989 by M. K. Brown. Reprinted by permission of Scholastic Inc.

Page 18: "Do-It-Yourself Experiments," from the book *Dr. Zed's Science Surprises* by Gordon Penrose. © 1989 Greey de Pencier Books. Used by permission of the publisher, Simon & Schuster Books for Young Readers, New York, NY 10020.

Page 28: *Tomás and the Library Lady* by Pat Mora. Text copyright © 1992 by Pat Mora. Reprinted by permission of Alfred A. Knopf, Inc.

Page 44: *My Dog and the Green Sock Mystery*. Text copyright © 1986 by David A. Adler. Illustrations copyright © 1986 by Dick Gackenbach. All rights reserved. Reprinted from *My Dog and the Green Sock Mystery* by permission of Holiday House.

Page 62: "Wait Little Joe" by Lessie Jones Little reprinted by permission of Philomel Books from *Children of Long Ago,* text copyright © 1988 by Weston Little, illustrations copyright © 1988 by Jan Spivey Gilchrist.

Page 64: *The Tortoise and the Hare.* Copyright © 1984 by Janet Stevens. All rights reserved. Reprinted from *The Tortoise and the Hare* by permission of Holiday House.

Page 82: "With Wrinkles and All" by Janet Stevens. Copyright © by Janet Stevens, 1991.

Page 86: *The Monkey and the Pea* by Nancy Ross Ryan. Copyright © by Nancy Ross Ryan, 1991.

Page 90: *The Big Fish Who Wasn't So Big* by Julius Lester. Copyright © by Julius Lester, 1991.

Page 96: "Animal Babies" from *Animals Learning* by Jane Burton. Text copyright © Jane Burton 1990. Photographs copyright © Jane Burton and Kim Taylor 1990. Reprinted by permission of Millbrook Press, Inc.

Page 102: "Robin Spied a Chubby Worm" from *Beneath a Blue Umbrella* by Jack Prelutsky, pictures by Garth Williams. Text copyright © 1990 by Jack Prelutsky. Illustrations copyright © 1990 by Garth Williams. Published by Greenwillow Books, a Division of William Morrow & Company, Inc. Reprinted by permission of William Morrow and Company, Inc.

Page 104: *Buffy's Orange Leash* by Stephen Golder and Lise Memling. Copyright © 1988 Gallaudet University. All rights reserved. Permission granted by Kendall Green Publications, an imprint of Gallaudet University Press.

Artists

Illustrations owned and copyrighted by the illustrator.
Debbie Drechsler, cover, 1–5, 117, 122–127
M. K. Brown, 6–17
Tina Holdcraft, 18–27
Cristina Ventoso, 28–43
Dick Gackenbach, 44–61, 120
Jan Spivey Gilchrist, 62–63
Janet Stevens, 64–85
Krystyna Stasiak, 86–89
Karen Barbour, 90–95, 120
Garth Williams, 102
Michele Warner, 104–116, 121

Photographs

Unless otherwise acknowledged, all photographs are the property of Scott Foresman.
Page 15: Courtesy of Joanna and Philip Cole
Pages 18–27: From the book *Dr. Zed's Science Surprises* by Gordon Penrose, © 1989 by permission of the publisher, Simon and Schuster, Inc., Books for Young Readers, New York.
Page 83: Courtesy of Janet Stevens
Pages 96–101: Photos by Jane Burton/Bruce Coleman Ltd.

Glossary

The contents of this glossary have been adapted from *My Second Picture Dictionary,* Copyright © 1990 Scott, Foresman and Company and *Beginning Dictionary,* Copyright © 1988 Scott, Foresman and Company.